COMMUNITY · CONNECTIONS

?

WHAT'S MINE IS YOURS
CHARITIES STARTED BY KIDS!
BY MELISSA SHERMAN PEARL AND DAVID A. SHERMAN

CHERRY LAKE
Publishing

Published in the United States of America by Cherry Lake Publishing
Ann Arbor, Michigan
www.cherrylakepublishing.com

Reading Adviser: Marla Conn MS, Ed., Literacy specialist, Read-Ability, Inc.

Photo Credits: Photos used with permission from What's Mine is Yours, Cover, 1, 5, 7, 9, 11, 13, 15, 17, 19, 21

**LIBRARY OF CONGRESS CATALOGING-IN-PUBLICATION DATA HAS BEEN
FILED AND IS AVAILABLE AT CATALOG.LOC.GOV**

Cherry Lake Publishing would like to acknowledge the
work of The Partnership for 21st Century Learning. Please
visit *www.p21.org* for more information.

Printed in the United States of America
Corporate Graphics

WHAT'S MINE IS YOURS

CONTENTS

HOW DO THEY HELP?

CHANGING THE WORLD CAN START WITH CHANGING CLOTHES

Every year, people **donate** over a billion pounds of used clothing. Donated clothing is sometimes sold for **proceeds** and sometimes shipped to other countries.

Paige Blake and Katie Easterly have been best friends since they were 5 years old. One thing they've always had in common is a love of fashion.

In 2015, Americans donated more than $250 billion to charities.

THINK!

Paige and Katie have been best friends for more than 10 years. How can you and your best friend do something to help others in the next 10 years?

5

To them, clothes are a creative form of expression.

In June 2012, two months before starting high school, the girls were cleaning out their closets. Many of the items were still in good shape and could be donated.

The girls wanted to be sure the clothing would remain local and benefit girls in their own **community**. They struggled to find such a place in California's Contra

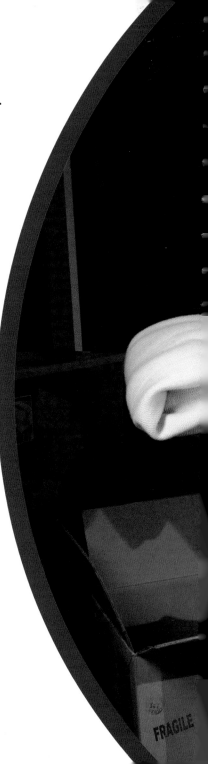

Many charities have their own resale shops and use the proceeds to fund other programs.

Think about the effects of empowering young people. When people feel good about themselves, they are way more likely to be successful and do good things.

Costa and Alameda Counties, where they lived.

Katie and Paige felt it was important that every girl has clothing that she loves and makes her feel confident when she wears it. They started What's Mine is Yours (WMIY) to provide "gently loved" clothing to **foster** girls in their community.

Each WMIY donation is hand-packaged and topped with a bow. Each package feels like a gift.

what's mine is yours™

Katie and Paige
accepted gently loved
clothing. What do
you think that means?
What sorts of clothes
would they take?
What do you think
they would not take?

9

FILLING THE BINS

The girls began by **distributing** bags to their neighbors and asking them for their daughters' old clothing that was still in good shape. Their goal was to find clothes for girls between 12 and 18 years old living within their community. The more people talked about this project, the more people started donating. Different high schools, middle schools, and even sports

WMIY collects "gently loved" clothing. This mean the clothing has no rips or stains.

SHIRTS

MAKE A GUESS!

Jeans with rips or stains aren't accepted by WMIY. But what can be done with old denim? Hint: Look at Blue Jeans Go Green online.

11

teams began holding donation drives for What's Mine is Yours.

Katie and Paige started making calls to local shelters and foster homes, in hopes of locating foster girls in need of clothing.

Wish lists were filled out by either a **social worker** or the girls they were helping. These lists were given to Paige and Katie, who turned the wishes into realities. They set up a store in a warehouse owned by Katie's grandfather. Twelve large

Katie and Paige use smartphones and tablets to view wishlists and stay organized.

LOOK!

What's Mine is Yours was a 2014 recipient of a grant from Tom's of Maine's 50 States for Good program. Take a look online and discover who else has earned such honors.

storage bins were labeled and filled with specific items. They would draw from these bins to pack all of the orders they had received.

In 2013, Katie and Paige created a one-day **boutique** featuring all of the gently loved clothing, calling it a "Pop-Up Event." Each of the agencies they work with is given a time slot when they can bring several girls to shop. The shoppers can browse on their own

WMIY wants to bring the joy of feeling strong and confident in your clothing to as many girls as possible.

LOOK!

What county do you live in? How many counties are in your state? What sort of needs exist in your county? Check your local library or search online for an answer.

15

or have Katie and Paige help them put outfits together. Shoppers often go from shy to **empowered** after the event.

How might feeling comfortable in your clothing make a difference in your actions?

Do you and your family donate your used clothes to charity? If so, do you know what the organization does with your clothes? Ask and find out!

17

SMALL DONATIONS, BIG DIFFERENCE

Today, WMIY works with more than 15 shelters and foster homes. Since WMIY began, the organization has donated over 17,500 pieces of clothing to more than 250 girls in their community.

Now that Katie and Paige are in college, they have high school students back home collecting and distributing donations.

WMIY also works with individuals to make sure every teenage girl in their community has the clothing they need.

Most charities do not accept very used clothing, towels, sheets, and stuffed animals. What can you do with these items? Ask your friends and family what they do.

Both Katie and Paige believe you can "never underestimate the power of giving." Starting WMIY was proof that need exists everywhere. There is almost always a need down the street or around the corner. You just have to keep your eyes open and be willing to help.

WMIY has gone from having 12 bins of clothing to over 100.

Start a gently loved clothing drive in your neighborhood and find a place to donate the goods. Remember, your drive doesn't have to be huge. Every little bit helps someone.

21

GLOSSARY

boutique (boo-TEEK) a small shop that sells fashionable clothes or other specialty items

community (kuh-MYOO-nih-tee) a group of people living in the same place

distributing (dih-STRIB-yoot-ing) giving out or delivering something

donate (DOH-nate) to give something to a charity or cause

empowered (em-POU-urd) stronger, more confident

foster (FAWS-tur) related to an orphaned, neglected, or delinquent child who is raised by someone other than his or her parent in that adult's home

proceeds (PROH-seedz) money earned from an event or activity

social worker (SOH-shuhl WUR-kur) someone who works to help provide aid to those who are disadvantaged

FIND OUT MORE

WEB SITES

www.bluejeansgogreen.org
By recycling worn denim into insulation, the Blue Jeans Go Green program keeps textile waste out of landfills and helps with building efforts in communities around the country.

www.clothesforthecausefundraising.com/clothing-fundraising -details
Learn about a West Coast program that recycles clothes (that are not gently loved), textiles, linens, stuffed animals, and a whole lot of other stuff to keep them out of landfills and raise money at the same time.

www.whatsmineisyours.us
Learn more about Paige and Katie and what they do.

INDEX

ABOUT THE AUTHORS

David Sherman and Melissa Sherman Pearl are cousins who understand and appreciate that you don't have to be an adult to make a difference.

24